Robert Jephson

Braganza

A Tragedy

Robert Jephson

Braganza
A Tragedy

ISBN/EAN: 9783337069582

Printed in Europe, USA, Canada, Australia, Japan

Cover: Foto ©ninafisch / pixelio.de

More available books at **www.hansebooks.com**

BRAGANZA.

A

TRAGEDY.

PERFORMED AT THE

THEATRE ROYAL

IN

DRURY-LANE.

WRITTEN BY

ROBERT JEPHSON, Esq.

LONDON:

Printed for T. EVANS, near York-Buildings in the Strand;
AND
T. DAVIES, in Ruffel-Street, Covent-Garden.
M DCC LXXV.
[Price One Shilling and Six-Pence.]

TO LADY

VISCOUNTESS NUNEHAM.

MADAM,

I HAVE many reasons to be flattered with the public reception of this Tragedy, yet I confess my solicitude for its reputation extends further.

Your Ladyship's having permitted me the honour of inscribing it to you, will in some measure gratify my ambition by recommending it to the reader, whose judgment is not influenced by the adventitious assistance of theatrical decorations and the graces of action.

Where your Ladyship's name appears as a patroness, merit will be expected; and where there is a wish to find any, probably none will pass unnoticed.

Whatever

Whatever motive may be affigned for this Addrefs, my principal purpofe will be fully anfwered if your Ladyfhip accepts it, as a teftimony of my gratitude for the favours I have received from the Noble Family to which you are fo happily united, and of the perfect efteem and refpect of

M A D A M,

Your Ladyfhip's

Much obliged and

Moft obedient

Humble Servant,

ROBERT JEPHSON.

Dublin Caftle,
Febr. 1775.

PROLOGUE.

Written by ARTHUR MURPHY, Efq.

SPOKEN BY MR. PALMER.

WHILE in thefe days of fentiment and grace
Poor comedy in tears refigns her place,
And fmit with novels, full of maxims crude,
She, that was frolick once, now turns a prude;
To her great end the tragic mufe afpires,
At Athens born, and faithful to her fires.
　The comic fifter in hyfteric fit,
You'd fwear, has loft all memory of wit.
Folly, for her, may now exult on high;
Feather'd by ridicule no arrows fly;
But if you are diftrefs'd, fhe's fure to cry.
She that could jig, and nick-name all heav'n's creatures,
With forrows not her own deforms her features;
With ftale reflections keeps a conftant pother;
Greece gave her one face, and fhe makes another;
So very pious, and fo full of woe,
You well may bid her " To a nunnery go."
Not fo Melpomene; to nature true
She holds her own great principle in view.
She, from the firft, when men her pow'r confeft,
When grief and terror feiz'd the tortur'd breaft,
She made, to ftrike her moral to the mind,
The ftage the great tribunal of mankind.
　Hither the worthies of each clime fhe draws,
Who founded ftates, or refcued dying laws;
Who, in bafe times, a life of glory led,
And for their country who have toil'd or bled;
Hither they come, again they breathe, they live,
And virtue's meed through ev'ry age receive.
　Hither the murd'rer comes, with ghaftly mien!
And the fiend confcience hunts him o'er the fcene.
None are exempted; all muft re-appear,
And even kings attend for judgement here;
Here find the day, when they their pow'r abufe,
Is a fcene furnifh'd to the tragic mufe.

Such

P R O L O G U E.

Such is her art, weaken'd perhaps at length,
And, while she aims at beauty, losing strength.
Oh! when resuming all her native rage,
Shall her true energy alarm the stage?

This night a bard---(our hopes may rise too high,
'Tis yours to judge;---'tis yours the cause to try)
This night a bard, as yet unknown to fame,
Once more, we hope, will rouze the genuine flame.
His; no French play;-- tame, polish'd, dull by rule!
Vigorous he comes, and warm from Shakespeare's school.
Inspir'd by him, he shews, in glaring light,
A nation struggling with tyrannic might;
Oppression rushing on with giant strides;
A deep conspiracy, which virtue guides;
Heroes, for freedom who dare strike the blow,
A tablature of honour, guilt and woe.
If on his canvafs nature's colours shine,
You'll praise the hand that trac'd the just design.

EPILOGUE.

EPILOGUE.

By a FRIEND.

SPOKEN BY MRS. YATES.

Is it permitted in this age severe,
For female softness to demand a tear?
Is it allow'd in such censorious days,
For female virtue to solicit praise?
Dares manly sense, beneath a tender form,
Presume to dictate, and aspire to warm?
May so unnatural a being venture
As a true heroine on the stage to enter?
No, says a wit, made up of French grimaces,
Yet self-ordain'd the high-priest of the graces.
Women are play-things for our idle hours,
Their souls unfinish'd, and confin'd their pow'rs;
Loquacious, vain, by slight attentions won,
By flattery gain'd, and by untruths undone.
Or should some grave great plan engage their minds,
The first caprice can give it to the winds;
And the chief statefwoman of all the sex
Grows nervous, if a fop or pimple vex.
  Injurious slanders!---in Louisa's air
Behold th' exemplar of a perfect fair;
Just, tho' aspiring; merciful, tho' brave;
Sincere, tho' politic; and tho' fond, no slave;
In danger calm, and smiling in success,
But as securing ampler means to bless.
  Nor think, as Zeuxis, for a faultless piece,
Cull'd various charms from various nymphs of Greece,
Our bard has center'd in one beauteous whole,
The rays that gleam thro' many a separate soul.
On Britain's and Ierne's shores he saw
The models of the fair he dar'd to draw;
True virtue in these isles has fix'd her throne,
And many a bright Louisa is our own.

PERSONS.

Don Juan, Duke of Braganza   Mr. Reddiſh.

Almada   —   — Mr. Aickin.

Ribiro   —   — Mr. Palmer.

Mendoza   —   — Mr. Brereton.

Antonio   —   — Mr. Wrighten.

Mello   —   — Mr. Wheeler.

Roderic   —   — Mr. Wright.

Ferdinand   —   — Mr. Norris.

Lemos   —   — Mr. Uſher.

Corea   —   — Mr. Hurſt.

Velaſquez, Miniſter of Spain   Mr. Smith.

Pizarro   —   — Mr. Davies.

Ramirez   —   — Mr. Packer.

Officer   —   — Mr. Keen.

Firſt Citizen   —   — Mr. Wright.

Second Citizen   — Mr. Griffiths.

Ines   —   — Mrs. Johnſton.

Louiſa, Dutcheſs of Braganza   Mrs. Yates.

Gentlemen, Attendants, Soldiers, &c.

SCENE, LISBON.

BRAGANZA;

A TRAGEDY.

ACT I.

SCENE I. *A Piazza.*

RIBIRO meeting a Spanish Officer conducting two Citizens bound. LEMOS and **COREA** *following RIBIRO at a little Distance.*

RIBIRO.

HOLD, officer——What means this spectacle?
Why lead you thus in fetters thro' the streets
These aged citizens?

OFFICER.
Behold this order.   [*shews a paper.*

RIBIRO.
I know the character. 'Tis signed Velasquez.

1st CITIZEN.
We have not mines of unexhausted gold
To feed rapacious Spain and stern Velasquez:
And wrung by hard exactions for the state——

OFFICER.
No more——I must not suffer it——

RIBIRO. *(pointing to the prisoners.)*
Pray, Sir——
See these white hairs, these shackles——Misery
May sure complain——You **are a soldier**, Sir,
Your mien bespeaks a brave one——

OFFICER.
I will **walk** by.
Detain them not too long——'Tis a harsh sentence.
[*Officer withdraws a little.*

B   2d CITIZEN.

2d CITIZEN.

O good Ribiro, what have we deferved,
That thefe rude chains fhou'd gall us?

RIBIRO.

What deferved!

1ft CITIZEN.

The little all our induftry had earn'd,
To fmooth the bed of ficknefs, nurfe old age,
And give a decent grave to our cold afhes,
Spain's hungry minions have already feized.——

RIBIRO.

I know the reft——Dry up thefe fcalding tears——
The hour of your deliv'rance is at hand:
——An arm more ftrong than fhuts your prifon doors,
Shall burft them foon, and give you ample vengeance.

CITIZENS.

May we indeed expect——

RIBIRO.

——Moft fure——But hufh——
Refume the femblance of this tranfient fhame,
And hide your hope in fadnefs——Brave Caftilian,
Thanks for this courtefy.   [*To the Officer, who returns.*

CITIZENS.

Lead on——Farewell.
                    [*Exeunt Guard and Citizens.*

LEMÓS *and* COREA *come forward to* RIBIRO.

RIBIRO.

Was that a fight for Lifbon?

LEMOS.

O fhame! fhame!
What crime cou'd they commit?——Old, helplefs, plunder'd——

RIBIRO.

——Even thoughts are crimes in this diftemper'd ftate.

They

They once had wealth as you have——Spain thought meet
To feize it——They (rafh men) have dar'd to murmur.
Velafquez here——our fcourge——King Philip's idol,
Whom Portugal muft bow to——mildly dooms them,
But to perpetual bondage for this treafon.

L E M O S.
We muft be patient——'Tis a curelefs evil.

R I B I R O.

Is patience then the only virtue left us ?
Come, come, there is a remedy more manly.

C O R E A.
Wou'd it were in our reach !

R I B I R O.
Look here, I grafp it.
[Laying his hand on his fword.
What turned to ftatues ! —Hence enfranchifement
If the quick fire that lately warm'd your breafts,
Already waftes to embers.——Am I rafh ?
We touch'd this theme before——You felt it then.
Wou'd I cou'd put a tongue in every ingot,
That now lies pil'd within your maffy ftores——
Your gold perhaps might move you——Spain will feize it,
Then bid you mourn the lofs in the next dungeon,
Or dig her mines for more——Is't not enough ?——
Inftruct me, Lemos, you, good Corea, teach me
This meeknefs fo convenient to our foes,
Or pierce this fwelling bofom.

L E M O S.
Who can teach it ?
'Tis not in art Ribiro——Know us better.
The canker difcontent confumes within,
And mocks our fmooth exterior.

C O R E A.
Hear me for both :
For all th' indignant hearts in Portugal——

B 2   If

If curfes fped like plagues and peftilence,
Thus wou'd I ftrike them at the towers of Spain.
May her fwoln pride burft like an empty bubble?
Diftraction rend her councils, route and fhame
Purfue her flying fquadrons——Tempefts fcatter
And whirlpools fwallow up her full man'd navies!
Bold infurrection fpread thro' all her ftates,
Shaking like pent-up winds their loofe allegiance!
All Europe arm, and every frowning king,
Point at one foe, and let that foe be Spain!

R I B I R O.

O be that curfe prophetic!——Here 'tis dangerous,
Nor will the time allow to tell you all.
But thus far reft affured;—I fpeak not rafhly—
A project is on foot, and now juft rip'ning,
Will give our indignation nobler fcope,
Than tears or curfes (priefts and womens weapons.)
All that fecures the event of great defigns,
Sage heads, firm hearts, and executing arms,
In formidable union league with us,
And chain capricious fortune to our ftandard.

L E M O S.

Say, can our aid promote this glorious caufe?

R I B I R O.

All private virtue is the public fund:
As that abounds, the ftate decays, or thrives;
Each fhou'd contribute to the general ftock,
And who lends moft, is moft his country's friend.

L E M O S.

O wou'd Braganza meet the people's wifh!

R I B I R O.

He is not yet refolved,—but may be won—
Cou'd I affure him men like you but wifh'd it,
(For well he knows and loves you)—Truft me, Lemos!
It wou'd do more to knit him to this caufe,
Than legions of our hot nobility.

C O R E A.

C O R E A.

We love his virtue—will fupport his rights—

R I B I R O.

Then fhew it by your deeds.—Your artizans
Are prompt, bold, hardy, fond of violence.
Alarm their flumb'ring courage, roufe their rage,
Wake their dulled fenfes to the fhame and fcorn
That hiffes in the ears of willing bondmen;
If they will hazard one bold ftroke for freedom,
A leader fhall be found, a brave—a juft one.
Anon expect me where the ivied arch
Rears the bold image of our late Braganza.
In fullen difcontent he feems to frown
As if ftill hoftile to the foes of Lifbon.
There we'll difcourfe at large—Almada comes—

L E M O S.

Is he a friend?

R I B I R O.

A firm one—No difhonour
E'er bow'd that rev'rend head—That mighty fpirit
When firft the oppreffor, like a flood, o'erwhelm'd us,
Rear'd high his country's ftandard and defied him.
—He comes to feek me—Lofe no time—Remember.

[Exeunt Lemos and Corea.

R I B I R O *alone.*

I fhou'd deteft my zeal, cou'd it be ftir'd
Againft the wholefome rigour of reftraint
Licentioufnefs made needful—But good Heaven!
Foul murders unprovok'd, delib'rate cruelty—
—The God within us muft rife up againft it.

Enter A L M A D A.

A L M A D A.

Well met Ribiro—What new profelytes?
Thy ardor every hour, or finds, or makes them.

R I B I R O.

No——thank the Spaniards for our proſelytes——
Scarce half an hour ago, two citizens
(My blood ſtill boils) by fell Velaſquez order
Were drag'd to priſon——

A L M A D A.

Spare my ſoul, Ribiro,
Superfluous deteſtation of that villain.

R I B I R O.

Knowing this way they were to paſs, I brought
Lemos and Corea (whom laſt night I founded)
That their own eyes might ſee the outrages,
Men of their order muſt expect to meet
From power that knows no bounds, and owns no law.

A L M A D A.

'Twas wiſely done; for minds of coarſe alloy
But bluntly feel the touch of others wrongs,
Tho' deep they take the impreſſion of their own.

R I B I R O.

By heav'n their fury bore a nobler ſtamp;
Their honeſt rage glow'd on their kindling cheeks,
Broke thro' the cold reſtraints of coward caution,
And ſwell'd even to an eloquence of anger.

A L M A D A.

'Tis well——But are they yet inform'd how near
Th' approaching hour, deciſive of our fate,
That gives us death or freedom——that the dawn——

R I B I R O.

Not yet——They ſtill believe the Duke at noon
But viſits Liſbon to command the march
Of our new levies, to the Spaniſh bounds;
Himſelf to follow ſtreight——Ere then I mean
Again to ſee them, and ſtill more to whet
The keeneſs of their hate againſt our tyrants.
——At leaſt a thouſand follow where they lead——

A L M A D A.

A L M A D A.

Their boldnefs well directed may do much.

R I B I R O.

That care be mine—I've ſtudied—and I know them ;
Inconſtant, ſanguine, eaſily inflam'd,
But like the nitrous powder uncompreſs'd,
Conſuming by the blaze nought but itſelf.
'Tis ours to charge the mine with deadly ſkill,
And bury uſurpation in the ruin.

A L M A D A.

I think we cannot fail—Our friends are firm.
Honour will bind the noble — Hope the weak,
And common intereſt all—The inſulting Spaniard
Broods over embryo miſchiefs, nor ſuſpects
The wretched worm conceals a mortal ſting
To pierce the haughty heel that tramples him.

R I B I R O.

How great will be our triumph, Spain's diſgrace,
When ev'ry miſchief that perfidious court
Has fram'd againſt Braganza's precious life,
Recoils on the contriver !

A L M A D A.

             Urge that home ;
Urge how the Duke's affection to his country,
His right unqueſtionable to her crown,
Firſt mark'd him for the victim of falſe Spain ;
That his commiſſion as high admiral,
His general's ſtaff, and all the lofty pomp
Of his high ſounding titles, were but meant
As gilded ſnares to invite him to his death.

R I B I R O.

Theſe truths, ſhameful to Philip, muſt be told ;
They will endear Don Juan to the people,
Will keep them waking, reſtleſs, and diſpos'd
To aid the glorious tumult of to-morrow.

A L M A D A.

My heart expands, and with a prophet's fire
Seizes the bright reversion of our hopes.
I see the genius of our realm restor'd,
And smiling lead him to his rightful throne.
No wild ambition, like a pamper'd steed,
O'erleaps the boundaries of law and reason,
And tramples every seed of social virtue :
But o'er the temp'rate current of his blood
The gentlest passions brush their breezy wings,
To animate, but not disturb the stream.
Such is his temper——The approaching hour
Demands perhaps a sterner.

R I B I R O.

Heaven still kind,
Has in his consort's breast struck deep the root
Of each aspiring virtue.——Bright Louisa,
To all the softness of her tender sex,
Unites the noblest qualities of man ;
A genius to embrace the amplest scheme
That ever swell'd the labouring statesman's breast ;
Judgment most sound, persuasive eloquence
To charm the froward and convince the wise ;
Pure piety without religion's drofs,
And fortitude that shrinks at no disaster.

A L M A D A.

She is indeed a wonder.——O Ribiro,
That woman was the spring that mov'd us all.
She canvass'd all our strength, urged all our wrongs,
Combin'd our force, and methodized our vengeance.
Taught us that ends which seem impossible
Are lost, or compass'd only by the means ;
That fortune is a false divinit.,
But folly worships what the wise man makes,
She turn'd our cold dejection to device,
And rous'd despondency to active valour.
My age delights to dwell on her perfections ——

R I B I R O.

R I B I R O.

And I could ever hear them——Virtue's praife
To honeft ears is mufic. —— But no more——
A noife comes this way, and that hurrying throng
Proclaims the upftart Minifter's approach.
This is the hour with faucy pageantry
Thro' our thin'd ftreets he takes his wonted round ;
Like the dire clapping of the harpy's wing,
To choak the frugal meal with bitter tears,
And fcare content from every humble board.
I will avoid him. But I go, proud man,
When next we meet to make my prefence dreadful.

                       [Exit Ribiro.

A L M A D A *alone.*

Honeft Ribiro!——To this hour my foul
Has kept her purpofe ; my firm foot has ne'er
Swerv'd from its path in Lifbon, nor fhall now
Give way to infolence.——Your country's dregs !

            [Looking towards the train of Velafquez.

Ye fupple fycophants ! Ay, cringe and beg
That he will tread upon your proftrate necks,
Or ride you like his mules.——Authority !
Thy worfhip'd fymbols round a villain's trunk
Provoke men's mockery, not their reverence.

O F F I C E R *entering.*

Make way there——room, room for the Minifter.
Know you the lord Velafquez comes this way ? *(To Almada.)*
Pray, Sir, give place.

A L M A D A.

          Officious varlet, off !
Let not thy fervile touch pollute my robe.
Can hirelings frown ?——

                        C

Enter VELASQUEZ *and* PIZARRO.——*The Magiſtrates of Liſbon with their Inſignia, Guards and Attendants preceding.*

VELASQUEZ. *(looking ſternly at Almada.)*

How! Am I then deſpiſed —
A tumult in my preſence :——Good, my lord,
It better wou'd become your gravity,
To ſet the fair example of obedience
To truſt and office, than inſtruct the rabble
In what they are the moſt prone to, feuds and faction.

ALMADA.

Moſt reverend admonition! Hold my ſpleen!
Ye golden coronets and ermin'd robes,
Bend from your ſtools, behold this wond'rous man,
This Luſitanian cenſor, this ſage Cato,
This conſul, with his lictors, rods and axes,
Reprove the boy, Almada, for his lightneſs!

PIZARRO.

Regard not his wild words, he's old and choleric.

VELASQUEZ. *(To his train.)*

Attend me at the citadel — Move on. [*Exeunt attendants.*
I know not whether to accuſe my fortune,
Or blame my own demerits ; brave Almada,
That ever when we meet, thy angry brow
Rebukes me with its frown, or keen reproach
Darts from thy tongue, and checks the forward wiſh
That fain wou'd court thy friendſhip and eſteem.

ALMADA.

Friendſhip with thee!——Is it ſo ſlight a boon ?
If ſuch deſerve the name, go ſeek for friends
Amidſt the deſp'rate crew whoſe only bond
Is the black conſcience of confederate crimes ;
Nor in prepoſt'rous union think to join
Integrity with guilt, and ſhame with honour.
Know me for what I am——thy foe profeſs'd.

Fall

Fall on thy knee—folicit Heaven for mercy,
And tell that feat of pride, thy obdurate he art,
Its laft, its only virtue is—remorfe.——

                           [*Exit Almada.*

Manent VELASQUEZ *and* PIZARRO.
VELASQUEZ.

  Go, hoary fool! preach to the whiftling winds,
I fcorn thy council, and defy thy hate.
'Tis time enough for lagging penitence,
When age, like thine, has quench'd ambition's flame.
Now nobler thoughts poffefs my active foul.
This haughty province firft fhall feel my weight,
And fince it fcorns my love, thro' fear obey me.

PIZARRO.

  Already all the power of Spain is thine,
The Vice Queen, Marg'ret, tho' of Auftrian blood,
Difcreet, firm, virtuous, complains in vain ;
You leave her but a regent's empty title,
While power is only yours :——And happier ftill,
Braganza fummon'd to attend the King,
Will foon cut off his country's only hope,
And leave no rival to obfcure thy luftre.
'Bate but the fhew and name of royalty,
Thou art already King.

VELASQUEZ.
                     The fhew, the name,
All that gives grace and awe to majefty
Shall foon be mine, Pizarro——Olivarez,
Whofe counfels rule the Efcurial, to my hand
Has long refign'd the reins of Portugal,
And dreams not (unfufpicious of my faith)
The Delegate, the creature of his breath,
Anon will bid defiance to his power,
And rank himfelf with monarchs.

PIZARRO.
                O take heed,
Confider, Sir, that power ftill awes the world——

                 C 2   VELASQUEZ,

VELASQUEZ.

My towering fortune rifes on a rock,
And firm as Atlas will defy the ftorm.
The purple cement of a Prince's blood
Shall ftrengthen its foundation.

PIZARRO.

Ha!

VELASQUEZ.

Braganza's.
—The precious mifchief fwells my exulting breaft,
And foon fhall burft its prifon.

PIZARRO.

Can it be?
I know thy dauntlefs temper mocks at fear,
And prudence guides thy daring.—But a Prince
Follow'd by faithful guards—encompafs'd round
With troops of gallant friends—the people's idol—

VELASQUEZ.

Is mortal, like the meaneft of his train,
And dies before to-morrow.—Ceafe to wonder—
But when this mighty ruin fhakes the realm,
Prepare like me, with well-diffembled grief,
To hide our real joy, and blind fufpicion.

[*Flourifh of trumpets.*

Thefe trumpets fpeak his entrance; never more
Such fprightly notes, nor fhout of joyful friends,
Pæan or choral fong fhall ufher him;
But fad folemnity of funeral pomp,
Mute forrow, mournful dirges, ghaftly rites,
Marfhal'd by death, in comfortlefs array,
Wait his cold relics to their fepulchre.

End of the Firft ACT.

ACT II.

SCENE I.

An Antichamber in the Duke of BRAGANZA's *Palace.*

RIBIRO, MENDOZA.

RIBIRO.

A Moment's pause, Mendoza! here appointed
By promise to the Duke at noon to wait him,
I could not mingle with his followers,
So saw it but in part——

MENDOZA.
   The air still rings
With loudest acclamations.

RIBIRO.
    Yes, Mendoza;
With joy I heard them——heard the vaulted sky
Echo Braganza.——'Twas no hireling noise,
No faction's roar of mercenary joy,
Sound without transport——but the heart-felt cry
Of a whole nation's welcome. Hear it Spain!
Proud usurpation hear it!

MENDOZA.
    The whole way
Was cover'd thick with panting multitudes,
That scarce left passage for their chariot wheels;
The trees were bent with people; ev'ry roof,
Dome, temple, portico, so closely fill'd,
The gazers made the wonder. Here and there

4

A discon-

A difcontented Spaniard ftalk'd along
Should'ring the crowd ; and with indignant fcorn
Turn'd up his fallow cheek in mockery.

R I B I R O.

We fhall retort their fcorn——Mark'd you the Duke ?
His mind is ever letter'd in his face.

M E N D O Z A.

Pleafure was mingled with anxiety,
Both vifible at once.   But, O what words
Can paint the angel form that grac'd his fide,
His bright Louifa ! like th' Olympian Queen,
When o'er her fragrant bofom Venus bound
Th' enchanting Ceftus——from her lucid eyes
Stream'd the pure beams of foft benevolence,
And glories more than mortal fhone around her.
Harmonious founds of dulcet inftruments
Swell'd by the breath, or fwept from tuneful wire,
Floated in air——while yellow Tagus burn'd
With prows of flaming gold ; their painted flags
In gaudy frolick fluttering to the breeze.
On to their palace thus the triumph came :
Alighted at the gate, the princely pair
Exprefs'd their thanks in filent dignity
Of gefture, far more eloquent than words ;
Then turn'd them from the throng——

R I B I R O.

Why this looks well.
The Duke will fure be rous'd to refolution
By this bright prefage of his coming glory.

M E N D O Z A.

With grief I learn he ftill is undetermin'd.
His fears prevail againft the public wifh ;
And thus the ill-pois'd fcale of our fair hopes,
Mounts light and unfubftantial.

R I B I R O.

R I B I R O.

          O you wrong him.
I know his noble nature——Juan's heart
Pants not with felfifh fear——His wife, his friends,
An infant family, a kingdom's fate,
More than his own, befiege his ftruggling foul;
He muft be more than man, who will not hear
Such powerful calls, and lefs, who can defpife them.

M E N D O Z A.

  Indeed I cannot wonder he's difturb'd,
But doubts are treafon in a caufe like this.

R I B I R O.

  Difmifs thefe fears——Louifa's gentle fway
Will fix him to our purpofe.   Night's chafte orb
Rules not the heavings of the reftlefs tide,
More fure than fhe with mild afcendancy
Can govern all his ebbs and flows of paffion.
But come, by this time the fond multitude
Have gaz'd away their longing, and retire.
Our greeting will be feafonable now.   [*Exeunt.*

S C E N E   II.

A magnificent Chamber in the Duke of BRAGANZA's *Palace.*
——The Duke fpeaking to LEMOS *and* COREA.——*Other*
Citizens at a little Diftance.

D U K E.

  No more kind countrymen——This goodnefs melts me.
What can I render back for all thefe honours?
This wond'rous prodigality of praife?
What but my life, whene'er your welfare afks it.

L E M O S.

  Heav'n guard that precious life for Portugal!
To you, as to a tutelary God,
This finking country lifts her fuppliant hands,

And certain of your strength, implores your arm
To raise her prostrate genius from the dust.

D U K E.

A private man, a subject like yourselves,
Bankrupt of power, though rich in gratitude——
The sense of what you suffer wrings my soul,
Nor makes your sorrows less.

D U T C H E S S.

     Much injur'd men
Whom love not fear should govern——from this hour
Know we espouse your cause——We have not hearts
Of aliens, to behold with passing glance
And cold indifference, the ruthless spoiler
Smile o'er the ravage of your fertile plains.
We feel the fetters that disgrace your limbs;
We mourn the vigour of your minds deprefs'd:
With horror we behold your gen'rous blood,
Drain'd by the insatiate thirst of ravening wolves.
If we have nature, we must feel your wrongs,
If we have power, redress them——

C O R E A.

     Matchless lady!
There spoke our rightful Queen, our better angel!
In us behold your servants, subjects, soldiers;
Though yet unpractis'd in the trade of war,
Our swords will find an edge at your command.

D U K E.

We neither doubt your courage nor your love,
And both perhaps ere long may meet the trial——
I would detain you——but our conference,
Might now be dangerous——Rank me with your friends,
And know I have a heart for Portugal.

       [*Exeunt Lemos, Corea, &c.*

          Manent

Manent DUKE *and* DUTCHESS.

DUTCHESS.

Why wears my Juan's brow that thoughtful cloud
Why thus with downcast look and folded arms?
When ev'ry other bosom swells with hope,
When expectation, like a fiery steed,
Anticipates the course, and pants to hear
The sprightly signal start him for the goal.
Think that the people from their leader's eye
Catch the sure omens of their future fate;
With his their courage falls, their spirits rise;
For confidence is conquest's harbinger.

DUKE.

Light of thy Juan's life! My soul's best joy?
Swifter than meteors glide, or wings of wind,
My nimble thoughts shoot thro' their whirling round:
A thousand cares distract this anxious breast.
To recompense the dark uncertainty
Of this dread interval, 'twixt now and morn,
Would ask whole years of happiness to come.
Now thou art mine, these faithful arms enfold thee;
But oh! to-morrow may behold thee torn
By barbarous ruffians from their fond embrace,
The flowing honours of that beauteous head,
May sweep a scaffold's dust, and iron death
Close in eternal sleep those radiant eyes
That beam with love and joy unutterable.

DUTCHESS.

O make me not your curse, as sure I must be,
The stain, the blot of your immortal fame,
If one soft passion like a languid spell,
Dissolve thy manly fortitude of soul,
And melt the prince and patriot in the husband.

DUKE.

That tender union is the healing balm,
The cordial of my soul——our destinies

Are twin'd together——Were my single life
The only forfeit of this perilous chance,
I'd throw it, like a heedless prodigal,
And wanton with my fortune——But alas!
More than the wealth of worlds is now at stake.
And can I hazard this dear precious pledge,
Venture my all of bliss on one bold cast,
Nor feel the conflict that now rends my heart?

DUTCHESS.

Why do you tremble?——These cold struggling drops——

DUKE.

——They fall for thee Louisa——my quell'd spirit
Avows its weakness there——

DUTCHESS.

     'Tis cruel fondness,
It wounds me deeply Juan.

DUKE.

     Witness honour!
Thy martial call ne'er found Braganza's ear
Cold, till this bitter moment.——I have met,
Nay courted death, in the steel'd files of war,
When squadrons wither'd as the giant trod;
Nor shrunk ev'n when the hardiest in the field
Have paused upon the danger——Here, I own,
My agonizing nerves degrade the soldier,
Ev'n to a coward's frailty——Should the sword
Which black destruction soon may wave o'er all,
(Avert it Heaven!) strike at thy precious life,
Should but one drop, forc'd by rude violence,
Stain that dear bosom, I were so accurs'd,
The outstretch'd arm of mercy could not save me.

DUTCHESS.

I have a woman's form, a woman's fears,
I shrink from pain and start at dissolution.
To shun them is great Nature's prime command;

Yet fummon'd as we are, your honour pledg'd,
Your own juft rights engag'd, your country's fate,
Let threat'ning death affume his direft form,
Let dangers multiply, ftill would I on,
Still urge, exhort, confirm thy conftancy,
And though we perifh'd in the bold attempt,
With my laft breath I'd blefs the glorious caufe,
And think it happinefs to die fo nobly.

D U K E.

O thou haft roufed me——From this hour I banifh
Each fond folicitude that hover'd round thee :
Thy voice,——thy looks——thy foul are heav'n's own fire.
'Twere impious but to doubt that pow'r ordain'd thee
To guide me to this glorious enterprize:

D U T C H E S S.

Thou fhalt be chronicl'd to lateft time,
Heaven's chofen inftrument to punifh tyrants.
The great reftorer of a nation's freedom !
Thou fhalt complete what Brutus but attempted.
Nor withering age, nor cold oblivion's fhade,
Nor envy's cank'rous tooth fhall blaft thy wreaths ;
But every friend to virtue fhall infcribe
To Juan's name eternal monuments.
But fee our friends approach——a-while I leave thee——
Remember ftill——thou muft be king or nothing.

[Exit Dutchef .

D U K E alone.

I will fupprefs th' emotions of my heart.
Quite to fubdue them is impoffible.

Enter RIBIRO and MENDOZA.

Welcome ye wakeful guardians of your country !
Had we in all the people's mighty mafs
But twenty fpirits match'd with you in virtue,
How might we bid defiance to proud Spain ;

How

How scorn the close disguise of secret councils,
And challenge their full force in open combat!

R I B I R O.

Led by Don Juan, can we doubt th' event?
All things conspire—Antipathy to Spain
Is here hereditary—'Tis nature's instinct,
'Tis principle, religion, vital heat.
Old men to list'ning sons with their last breath
Bequeath it as a dying legacy.
Infants imbibe it at the mother's breast.
It circles with their blood, spreads with their frame.
Its fountain is the heart, and till that fails
The stream it fed can never cease to flow.

M E N D O Z A.

That furious impulse gives the spleen of fiends
To softest tempers, the unpractis'd arm
Sinews with lion's strength, and drives us on
Resistless as the sweeping whirlwind's force.

D U K E.

All is propitious! Every post is fill'd
With officers devoted to our service:
Already in their hearts they own my title,
And wait but for our orders to proclaim it.

Enter A L M A D A.

D U K E.

Come to my breast, my sage admonisher!
The tutor and example of my arms!
The proud Iberian soon shall feel their force;
And learn from Juan's sword to venerate
The fame of brave Almada.

A L M A D A.

                              Thus my prince,
Thus did I hope to find thee. Hence no more
Shall hard exactions grind the prostrate people;

Our

Our gentry to their provinces confin'd
Languish no more in shameful circumscription;
No more our ancient noblemen be stripp'd
Of all but empty titles, tinsel names
Like tarnish'd gold on rags to mock the wearer!
Our posts of eminence no more be filled
With upstart strangers, or the sordid lees
Of base plebian natives——

D U K E.

               My impatient breast,
Full of the expected joy, like a young bridegroom,
Upbraids the lazy hours that lag between
My wishes and enjoyment——The onset is——

A L M A D A.

When St. Lazar beats five, about that hour
We'll welcome the sun's rising with an offering
More glorious than the Persians Hecatomb.

R I B I R O.

At night your friends assemble with Almada
In dreadful secrecy — Then with rais'd arm
We rush to cancel our long debt to vengeance,
And glut our thirsty blades with Spanish gore.

A L M A D A.

If we suspend the blow beyond to-morrow
All may be lost — Three thousand veterans
Lye canton'd on the river's southern side;
Should our design be known, they will be call'd
To reinforce the posts, and guard the city.
Adieu then to our dream of liberty!
We rivet closer chains on Portugal,
And drag the doom of traytors on ourselves.

Enter DUTCHESS.

DUTCHESS.

Sufpend your confultations for a moment,
Within the minifter of Spain attends ;
Forgive th' officious love of your Louifa :
No ftranger to his arts, fhe warns her Juan——

DUKE.

I know he comes in folemn mockery
To make a hollow tender of his fervice
With moft obfequious falfhood.

DUTCHESS.

                    My beft Lord,
Hold ftricteft watch on all your words and motions;
Guard every look, with that difcerning villain ;
Subtle, infiduous, falfe, and plaufible ;
He can with eafe affume all outward forms,
Seem the moft honeft, plain, fincere good man,
And keep his own defigns lock'd clofe within,
While with the lynx's beam he penetrates
The deep referve of every other breaft.

DUKE.

I too will wear my vizor in the fcene,
And play the dupe I am not.——Friends, farewell !
Perhaps ere morning we may meet again——
The hour is fix'd, Louifa ;——all prepar'd——

DUTCHESS.

Then this is our laft night of flavery——
A brighter æra rifes with the dawn.   [*Exit Duke.*
If we may dare without impiety
To challenge heavenly aid, and fwell the breaft
With confidence of more than mortal vigour,
Can Heaven ftand neuter in a caufe like this ?
Or favour fraud, oppreffion, cruelty ?
——Now gentle friends I am a fuitrefs to you.

                              A L M A D A.

A L M A D A.

You are our sovereign, madam——'tis your right,
Not to sollicit but command our duty.

D U T C H E S S.

Think me not light, capricious, variable,
If I who urg'd ye to this bold attempt,
And ever when your anger seem'd to cool
Pour'd oil to wake the flame and feed its blaze,
Now supplicate with milder earnestness
And strive to allay its fury.

A L M A D A.

             Speak your pleasure!
The obedience of our hearts will follow it !

D U T C H E S S.

I know the measure of your wrongs would license,
Nay justify the wild excess of vengeance ;
Yet in the headlong rage of execution,
Think rather what your mercy may permit
Than what their crimes deserve who feel your justice.
O ! follow not the example we abhor,
Nor let those weapons justice consecrates
Be dy'd with drops drawn from the bleeding breast
Of reverend age, or helpless innocence.
Wilt thou take heed Almada ?

A L M A D A.

             Fear not, madam,
All mercy not injurious to our cause,
Ev'n Spaniards, as they are men, from men may challenge.
For Indus' wealth I wou'd not stain this sword,
Sacred to honour, in the guiltless blood
Of unoffending wretches——rest secure,
A prostrate and defenceless enemy,
Has stronger guards against a brave man's wrath,
Than tenfold brass, or shields of adamant.

D U T C H E S S.

DUTCHESS.

Gen'rous Almada! well doft thou inftruct——
Soft pity is not more akin to love
Than to true fortitude.——Thy foft youth, Mendoza,
Need not be tutor'd to humanity.

MENDOZA.

Heav'n and my confcious foul bear witnefs for me,
That not to fatiate any private malice,
But for the general good, I ftand engag'd
In this great compact.——'Twere a coward's vengeance
To turn a facrifice to maffacre,
And practice while I punifh cruelty.

RIBIRO.

Till fortune give one victim to my rage,
Compaffion and this bofom muft be ftrangers,
No fanctuary, nor interceding prayers,
Nor wings of angels ftretch'd to cover him,
Shall fave that monfter from the doom he merits.

DUTCHESS.

You mean the minifter of Spain, Velafquez.

RIBIRO.

I mean the minifter of hell, Velafquez,
That cool deliberate executioner ;
If he efcape, may this good arm rot off,
All worthy thoughts forfake, and fcorn purfue me :
Write boafter on my forehead——let my name
Blifter the tongue that fpeaks it.——Infamy
Be here my portion, endlefs pains hereafter.

DUTCHESS.

O would that facrifice might expiate !——

RIBIRO.

Pardon the rafh effufion of my zeal ;
It deals too much in words.

DUTCHESS.

DUTCHESS.

Not so, Ribiro,
Thy anger has a licenfe;—and thy zeal
We know is generous, not fanguinary.

ALMADA.

Madam, we take our leave—good angels guard you!
We go to prove our duty in your fervice.
The homage of our hearts has long been yours,
And foon you fhall receive it from our knees.

DUTCHESS.

Believe me, friends, your loves are written here,
In characters no time can e'er efface.

[*Exeunt Almada, Ribiro and Mendoza.*

DUTCHESS *alone*.

And may the mighty fpirits of paft times
Rais'd by defert to bright immortal thrones,
Sufpend awhile their tafk of heav'nly praife
In miniftry unfeen to hover round them!
Protect afpiring virtue like their own,
And in their bofoms breathe refiftlefs ardour!   [*Exit.*

End of the Second ACT.

E   ACT

A　C　T　III.

S C E N E　I.

The Apartments of VELASQUEZ, *in the Palace of the Vice-Queen.*

VELASQUEZ, PIZARRO.

PIZARRO.

YOU feem difturb'd——

VELASQUEZ.

With reafon——dull Braganza
Muft have been tutor'd——At our interview
I practis'd every fupple artifice
That glides into man's bofom——The return
Was blank referve, ambiguous compliment,
And hatred thinly veil'd by ceremony.

PIZARRO.

Might I prefume——

VELASQUEZ.

Pizarro, I am ftung——
His father Theodofius, that proud Prince,
Who durft avow his enmity to Philip,
And menac'd thunders at my deftin'd head,
With all his empty turbulence of rage
Cou'd never move me like the calm difdain
Of this cold blooded Juan.

PIZARRO.

P I Z A R R O.

Then, my Lord,
Your purpose holds.

V E L A S Q U E Z.

It does—I will dispatch
This tow'ring Duke, who keeps the check of Spain
Pale with perpetual danger.

P I Z A R R O.

For what end ?
Unconscious of his fate, he blindly speeds
To find a grave in Spain—Why then resolve
To spill that blood, which elsewhere will be shed
Without your crime or peril ?

V E L A S Q U E Z.

That's the question.
Were I assur'd they meant his death, 'twere needless :
But when they draw him once from Portugal,
Where only he is dangerous, then perhaps
Their fears, or lenity may let him live ;
And while he lives, my fiery course is check'd,
My sun climbs slowly, never can ascend
To its meridian brightness.

P I Z A R R O,

Still, my Lord,
My short lin'd wisdom cannot found your depth.

V E L A S Q U E Z.

I mean to tell thee all, for thou may'st aid me,
And thy tried faith deserves my confidence.

P I Z A R R O.

I am your own for ever—Your kind hand,
Bounteous beyond my merit, planted here
Favours innumerable.—

VELASQUEZ.

—Think them little—
An earnest, not the acquittal of my love.
The enormous wealth of Juan's royal house,
His large domains, extended influence,
His numerous vassals so have swell'd his state,
That were his means but push'd to one great end;
How easy might he wrest this realm from Spain,
And brave King Philip's rage?

PIZARRO.

Good careless prince!
Mild and uxorious! No ambitious dream
Disturbs his tranquil slumber—

VELASQUEZ.

Just his nature!
On household wing he flutters round the roof,
That with the princely eagle might have soar'd
And met the dazzling sun. Now by his death
(My engine cannot fail, this night he meets it)
His wealth, his mightiness, his followers
Become Louisa's dower—What think'st thou now?
Cou'd I but win her to accept my hand,
(And much my art will move, and more my power)
Might not our union, like the impetuous course
Of blending torrents, break all feeble mounds
Spain cou'd oppose to bar me from the crown?
That once obtain'd, let Olivarez rail,
Let his inglorious master call me traitor,
I'll scorn their idle fury.

PIZARRO.

Still I fear
Louisa's heart, cold and impenetrable,
To all but Juan's love, will own no second,

Tho'

Tho' big ambition fwells her female breaſt
Beyond the fex's foftnefs.

V E L A S Q U E Z.

My hope refts
Even on that favourite paffion—Grief at firſt
Will drive her far from love—A fecond flame
Perhaps may ne'er rekindle in her heart;
Yet, give her momentary frenzy fcope,
It waſtes itſelf; ambition then regains
Its wonted force and winds her to my lure—
But come—I muſt not lofe thefe precious moments,
The Fates are bufy now—What's yet untold,
There place thyfelf and learn—Take heed you move not.

[*Pizarro retires.*

Without there! Ho!

Enter an OFFICER.

O F F I C E R.

What is your lordſhip's pleafure?

V E L A S Q U E Z.

Attends the monk, Ramirez?

O F F I C E R.

He does, my lord.

V E L A S Q U E Z.

Conduct him in and leave us.

Enter R A M I R E Z.

You are welcome,
Moſt welcome, reverend father—Pray draw near—
We have a bufinefs for your privacy,
Of an efpecial nature—The circling air
Shou'd not partake it, nor the babbling winds,

Let

Left their invisible wings disperse one breath
Of that main secret, which thy faithful bosom
Is only fit to treasure.

RAMIREZ.

Good my lord,
I am no common talker.

VELASQUEZ.

Well I know it,
And therefore chose thee from the brotherhood,
Not one of whom but wou'd lay by all thoughts
Of earth and Heaven, and fly to execute
What I, the voice of Spain, commission'd him.

RAMIREZ.

Vouchsafe directly to unfold your will,
My deeds, and not my words, must prove my duty.

VALESQUEZ.

Nay, trust me, cou'd they but divine my purpose,
The holiest he, that wastes the midnight lamp
In prayers and penance, wou'd prevent my tongue
And hear me thank the deed, but not persuade it.
Therefore, good friend, 'tis not necessity,
That sometimes forces any present means,
And chequers chance with wisdom, but free will,
The election of my judgment and my love,
That gives thy aptness this pre-eminence.

RAMIREZ.

The state, I know, has store of instruments,
Like well-rang'd arms in ready order plac'd,
Each for its several use.

VELASQUEZ.

Observe me well;
Think not I mean to snatch a thankless office;

Who ferves the ftate, while I direct her helm,
Commands my friendfhip, and his own reward.
Say, can you be content in thefe poor weeds
To know no earthly hopes beyond a cloyfter?
But ftretch'd on mufty matts in noifome caves,
To roufe at midnight bells, and mutter prayers
For fouls beyond their reach, to fenfelefs faints?
To wage perpetual war with nature's bounty?
To blacken fick men's chambers, and be number'd
With the loath'd leavings of mortality,
The watch-light, hour-glafs, and the naufeous phial?
Are thefe the ends of life? Was this fine frame,
Nerves exquifitely textur'd, foft defires,
Afpiring thoughts, this comprehenfive foul,
With all her train of god-like faculties
Given to be funk in this vile drudgery?

R A M I R E Z.

Thefe are the hard conditions of our ftate.
We fow our humble feeds with toil on earth,
To reap the harveft of our hopes in Heaven.

V A L E S Q U E Z.

Yet wifer they who truft no future chance,
But make this earth a Heaven. Raife thy eyes
Up to the temporal fplendors of our church;
Behold our priors, prelates, cardinals;
Survey their large revenues, princely ftate,
Their palaces of marble, beds of down,
Their ftatues, pictures, baths, luxurious tables,
That fhame the fabled banquets of the gods.
See how they weary art, and ranfack nature
To leave no tafte, no wifh ungratified.
Now—if thy fpirit fhrink not—I can raife thee
To all this pomp and greatnefs.—Pledge thy faith,
Swear thou wil't do this thing—whate'er I urge,
—And Lifbon's envied crozier fhall be thine,

R A M I R E Z.

R A M I R E Z.

This goodnefs, fo tranfcending all my hopes,
Confounds my aftonifh'd fenfe.—Whate'er it be
Within the compafs of man's power to act,
I here devote me to the execution.

V E L A S Q U E Z.

I muft not hear of confcience and nice fcruples,
Tares that abound in none but meagre foils,
To choak the afpiring feeds of manly daring :
Thofe puny inftincts, which in feeble minds,
Unfit for great exploits, are mifcall'd virtue——

R A M I R E Z.

Still am I loft in dark uncertainty ;
And muft for ever wander, till thy breath
Deign to difpel the impenetrable mift,
Fooling my fight that ftrives in vain to pierce it.

V E L A S Q U E Z.

You are the Duke of Braganza's confeffor,
And fame reports him an exact obferver
Of all our churches' holy ceremonies.
He ftill is won't whene'er he vifits Lifbon,
Ere grateful flumber feal his pious lids,
With all due reverence, from fome prieftly hand
To take the myftic fymbol of our faith.

R A M I R E Z.

It ever was his cuftom, and this night
I am commanded to attend his leifure
With preparation for the folemn act.

V E L A S Q U E Z.

I know it——Take *(gives him a box.)* thou this—It holds a water
Of fovereign virtue to enfranchife fouls,
Too righteous for this world, from mortal cares.

A monk

A monk of Milan mix'd the deadly drug,
Drawn from the quinteffence of noxious plants,
Minerals and poifonous creatures, whofe dull bane
Arrefts the nimble current of life's tide,
And kills without a pang.

R A M I R E Z.

I knew him well,
The Carmelite Caftruccio, was it not?

V E L A S Q U E Z.

The fame, he firft approv'd it on a wretch
Condemn'd for murder to the ling'ring wheel.
This night commit it to Braganza's lips.
Had he a heart of iron, giant ftrength,
The antidotes of Pontus—All were vain,
To ftruggle with the venom's potency.

R A M I R E Z.

This night, my lord?

V E L A S Q U E Z.

This very night, nay, fhrink not,
Unlefs thou mean'ft to take the lead in death,
And pull thy own deftruction on thy head.

R A M I R E Z.

Give me a moment's paufe—A deed like this—

V E L A S Q U E Z.

Should be at once refolv'd and executed.
Think'ft thou I am a raw unpractis'd novice,
To make thy breaft a partner to the truft,
And not thy hand accomplice of the crime?
Why 'tis the bond for my fecurity :
Look not amaz'd, but mark me heedfully.
Thou haft thy choice—difpatch mine enemy.
The means are in thy hand—be fafe and great,

Or

Or inftantly prepare thee for a death
Which nothing but compliance can avert.

R A M I R E Z.

Numbers I know even thus have tafted death,
But fure imagination fcarce can form
A way fo horrid, impious!

V E L A S Q U E Z.

How's this, How's this!
Hear me, pale mifcreant, my rage once rous'd,
That hell thou dread'ft this moment fhall receive thee.
Look here and tremble——   [*Draws a dagger and feizes him.*

R A M I R E Z.

My lord be not fo rafh,
Your fury's deaf——Will you not hear me fpeak?
By ev'ry hope that cheers, all vows that bind,
Whatever horror waits upon the act,
Your will fhall make it juftice——I'm refolv'd.

V A L A S Q U E Z.

No trifling, Monk——take heed, for fhould'ft thou fail——.

R A M I R E Z.

Then be my life the forfeit——My obedience
Not only follows from your high command,
But that my bofom fwells againft this Duke
With the full fenfe of my own injuries.——

V E L A S Q U E Z.

Enough——I thank thee——Let me know betimes
How we have profper'd.   Hence, retire with caution,
Deferve my favour, and then meet me boldly. [*Exit Ramirez.*
'Tis done——His doom is feal'd——Come forth Pizarro.
[*Pizarro comes forward.*
Is't not a fubtle mifchief?

PIZARRO.

PIZARRO.

Past all praise,
The holy tool had qualms.

VELASQUEZ. *(Pointing to his dagger.)*

But this dispell'd them,
And fortified the coward by his fears.
His work perform'd, I mean to end him too. —
Say, is my barge prepar'd as I commanded?

PIZARRO.

All is prepar'd, my Lord.

VELASQUEZ.

The friends of Juan,
(I'll tell thee as we pass) they shall not long
Survive to lift their crests so high in Lisbon.   [*Exeunt.*

SCENE *changes to the Castle of* ALMADA.

Enter ALMADA *and an Attendant.*

ALMADA.

Good Perez, see that none to night have entrance
But such whose names are written in that roll,
And bid your fellows from the northern tower,
Chuse each a faulchion, and prepare to follow
Where I at dawn will lead.

ATTENDANT.

I will, my Lord.

ALMADA.

Wait near the gate thyself, nor stir from thence
Without my summons.

A T T E N D A N T.

Truſt my vigilance. [*Exit Attendant.*

A L M A D A *alone.*

Now raylefs midnight fl'ngs her fable pall
Athwart the horizon, and with pond'rous mace
In dead repofe weighs down o'er-labour'd nature,
While we, the bufy inftruments of fate,
Unmindful of her feafon, wake like ghofts,
To add new horrors to the fhadowy fcene.

To him enter feveral of the Duke of BRAGANZA'S *Friends.*

A N T O N I O.

Health to Almada.

A L M A D A.

Thus to meet, Antonio!
Is the beft health, the foundnefs of the mind.
Better at this dark hour to embrace in arms
Thus girt for manly execution, friend!
Than in the mazes of the wanton dance,
Or revelling o'er bowls in frantic mirth,
To keep inglorious vigils.

A N T O N I O.

True, my Lord.

Enter R I B I R O *with* L E M O S *and* C O R E A.

A L M A D A. *(to Ribiro.)*

O foul of honour, ever, ever conftant.
Thefe are the worthy citizens, our friends——

R I B I R O. *(Prefenting Lemos and Corea.)*

And fuch as laurell'd Rome might well have own'd

·3   Worthy

Worthy to fill her magifterial chairs,
When reverence bow'd to virtue tho' untitled.

ALMADA.

As fuch I take their hands, nay more as fuch,
Their grateful country will rejoice to own them.
Are we all met?

ANTONIO.

Mendoza is not here,
Nor Roderic, and Mello too is abfent.

ALMADA.

They were not wont to be thus waited for.

RIBIRO.

Anon they will be here,—mean time proceed,
They know their place already—

ALMADA.

Why we meet,
Is not to canvafs our opprobrious wrongs,
But to redrefs them.—Yet as trumpets found,
To roufe the foldier's ardor,—fo the breath
Of our calamities will wake our fires,
And fan them to fpread wide the flame of vengeance.
'Tis not my gift to play the orator,
But in plain words to lay our ftate before you.
—Our tyrant's grandfire, whofe ambition claim'd,
And firft ufurp'd Braganza's royal rights,
My blood eftablifh'd his detefted fway.
Old Tagus blufh'd with many a crimfon tide,
Sluic'd from the nobleft veins of Portugal.
The exterminating fword knew no diftinction.
Princes, and prelates, venerable age,

Matrons,

Matrons, and helpleſs virgins fell together,
'Till cloy'd and ſick of ſlaughter, the tir'd ſoldier
With grim content flung down his reeking ſteel,
And glutted rage gave truce to maſſacre.

R I B I R O.

Nor paſs'd the iron rod to milder hands
Thro' two ſucceeding reigns——With cruel zeal
The barbarous offspring emulate their ſire,
And track his bloody footſteps in our ruin.

A L M A D A.

Now mark how happily the time conſpires,
To give our great atchievement permanence;
——Spain is not what ſhe was, when Europe bow'd
To the fifth Charles, and his degenerate ſon.
When, like a torrent ſwell'd by mountain floods,
She ſwept the neighbouring nations with her arms,
And threaten'd thoſe remote,——contracted now
Within an humble bed, the thrifty urn,
Of her exhauſted greatneſs, ſcarce can pour
A lazy tide thro' her own mould'ring ſtates;

R I B I R O.

Yes the Coloſſus totters, every blaſt
Shakes the ſtupendous maſs and threats its downfall.

Enter M E N D O Z A.

M E N D O Z A.

Break off——break off——the fatal ſnare is ſpread,
And death's pale hand aſſiſts to cloſe the toil.

A L M A D A.

Whence this dread greeting?——Ha——thy alter'd cheek
Wears not the enſign of this glowing hour.

M E N D O Z A.

M E N D O Z A.

The fcream of night owls, or the ravens croak
Wou'd better fuit the baleful news I bring,
Than the known accents of a friendly voice.
—We are undone—betray'd—

A L M A D A.

Say'ft thou—betray'd?

M E N D O Z A.

Our tower is fap'd—the high rais'd fabric falls
To crufh us with the ruin —What avails
The full maturity of all our hopes?
This glorious league—the juftice of our caufe?—
—High Heaven might idly thunder on our fide,
If traitors to ourfelves.—

A L M A D A.

Ourfelves—Oh fhame!
I'll not believe it —What perfidious flaves—

M E N D O Z A.

Two whom we thought the finews of our ftrength,
Don Roderic and Mello.—

R I B I R O.

Lightnings blaft them!
May infamy record their daftard names,
And vulgar villains fhun their fellowfhip—
Thefe hot, loud brawlers—

M E N D O Z A.

Are the flaves of Spain,
And bargain for the price of perfidy.—
On to the wharf with quick impatient ftep,
I faw Velafquez prefs, and in his train

Thefe

These lurking traitors.—Now, even now, they cross
The ebbing Tagus in the tyrant's barge,
And hasten to the fort.—The troops of Spain,
Even while we speak, are summon'd to the charge,
And mark us for their prey.

A L M A D A.

                    Nay then, 'tis past.
Malignant fortune, when the cup was rais'd
Close to our lips, has dash'd it to the ground.

R I B I R O.

  This unexpected bolt strikes flat our hopes,
And leaves one dreary desolation round us.
I see their hangmen muster.—wolf-ey'd cruelty,
Grimly sedate, glares o'er her iron hoard
Of racks, wheels, engines, feels her axe's edge
Licks her fell jaws, and with a monster's thirst,
Already drinks our blood.

M E N D O Z A.

                    There's not a pang
That rends the fibres of man's feeling frame,
No vile disgrace, that even in thought o'er-spreads
The cheek with burning crimson, but her hate
Ingenious to devise, and sure to inflict
In keenest agony will make us suffer.

A L M A D A.

  Wou'd that were all—Our dismal scene must close;
Nature o'er power'd at length will leave her load,
And baffle persecution.—But O, Portugal!
Alas! unhappy country! Where's the bourn
Can mark the extent of thy calamities.
Like winter's icy hand our luckless end
Will freeze the source of future enterprize:

                                        Oppression

Oppreffion then o'er the devoted realm
Erect and bold will ftalk with tenfold ravage.
There, there alone, this breaft is vulnerable;
Thefe are the wheels that wrench, the racks that tear me.

A N T O N I O.

But are there left no means to elude the danger?
Why do we linger here?——Why not refolve
To fave ourfelves by flight?

M E N D O Z A.
Impoffible!
The guards no doubt are fet——the port is bar'd.

A L M A D A.

Fly Lemos to the people, and reftrain
Their generous ardor.——It wou'd now break forth
Ufelefs to us, and fatal to themfelves.   [Exit Lemos.
You to the Duke, Ribiro!——In our names,
(Perhaps our laft requeft) by our loft fortunes,
By all our former friendfhip, O conjure him
To fave our richeft treafure from the wreck,
Nor hazard in a defperate enterprize
His country's laft beft hope, his valued life.

R I B I R O.

Support him Heaven, and arm his piety
To bear this fad viciffitude with patience.   [Exit Ribiro.

A L M A D A.

And yet we will not meet in vain, brave friends;
We came with better hopes, refolv'd like men
To ftruggle for our freedom.——What remains?
A greater power than mortals can arraign,
Has otherwife decreed it.——Speak, my brothers,
Now doubly dear in ftern adverfity;
Say, fhall we glut the fpoiler with our blood,
Submit to the vile infults of their law,

G   To

To have our honeſt duſt by the ruffian hands
Given to the winds——Is this the doom that waits us ?

M E N D O Z A.

Alas what better doom ? To aſk for mercy
Were ignominious, to expeĉt it bootlefs.

A L M A D A.

To aſk for mercy——cou'd Spain ſtretch my life
To years beyond the telling, for one tear,
One word, in ſign of ſorrow, I'd diſdain it.
Death ſtill is in our pow'r——and we'll die nobly,
As ſoldiers ſhou'd do, red with well earn'd wounds,
And ſtretch'd on heaps of ſlaughter'd enemies.

[*Exeunt ſeverally.*

End of the Third A C T.

ACT IV.

SCENE I.

A Chamber in the Duke of BRAGANZA's *Palace.*

DUTCHESS *alone.*

O Thou supreme disposer of the world !
If from my childhood to this awful now,
I've bent with meek submission to thy will,
Send to this feeble bosom one blest beam
Of that bright emanation, which inspires
True confidence in thee, to calm the throbs
That heave this bosom for my husband's safety,
And with immortal spirit to exalt
Above all partial ties our countries love.

To her enter RIBIRO *hastily.*

RIBIRO.

Where is the Duke ? O pardon, gracious madam.

DUTCHESS.

What means this haste and these distracted looks ?

RIBIRO.

Detain me not—but lead me to my Lord.—
His life, perhaps—nay, your—

DUTCHESS.

His life—O heavens !
Tell me, Ribiro—speak—

G 2   RIBIRO.

R I B I R O.

                Too foon, alas
You'll hear it——Afk not now dear lady
What I've fcarce breath to utter——Where's the Duke?

D U T C H E S S.

  This moment with his confeffor retir'd
I left him in his clofet.

R I B I R O.

                ——'Tis no time——
All muft give place to this dire urgency.
Even while we fpeak——A moment's precious now.——
He muft be interrupted——Guide me to him.

D U T C H E S S.

Sufpenfe is ling'ring death.——Come on, I'll lead you.
                                          [*Exeunt.*

Ente R A M I R E Z.

R A M I R E Z.

  O welcome interruption——Pitying Heaven
A while at leaft arrefts the murd'rous deed,
And gives a moment's refpite from damnation.
——Is there a hell beyond this war of confcience?
My blood runs backward, and my tottering knees
Refufe to bear their facrilegious load.
Methought the ftatues of his anceftors,
As I pafs'd by them, fhook their marble heads;
His father's picture feem'd to frown in wrath,
And its eye pierce me, while I trembling ftood
Affaffin like before it——Hufh——I'm fummon'd.

Re-enter DUTCHESS.

DUTCHESS.

Get you to rest good father—Fare you well.
Some unexpected bufinefs of the ftate
Demands my Lord's attention—For this night
Your holy function muft be unperform'd
Till more convenient feafon.

RAMIREZ.

          Holy function!   [*afide.*
I humbly take my leave, and will not fail
To recommend you in my prayers to Heaven.

                [*Exit Ramirez*

DUTCHESS.

The Heavens I fear are fhut and will not hear them.
—Now gufh my tears—now break at once my heart!
While in my Juan's prefence, I fupprefs'd
The burfting grief—But here give nature way!
Is there a hope—Oh no—All horrible—
My children too—Their little lives—My hufband—
I conquer'd his reluctance—I perfuaded
By every power his boundlefs paffion gave me—
I thought it virtue too—Myfterious Heaven?—
Then I, and only I, have work'd his ruin.

Enter DUKE.

DUKE.

Alas my love, why muft thy Juan feek thee?
Why do'ft thou fhun me at this aweful moment?
The few fad hours our deftiny permits,
Shou'd fure be fpent together.

DUTCHESS.

         Muft we part then?
               DUKE.

DUKE.

I fear we muſt for ever in this world,
Till that great power who faſhion'd us in life,
Unites us once again no more to ſever;
In thoſe bleſt regions of eternal peace,
Where ſorrow never enters, where thy truth,
Thy unexampl'd fortitude and ſweetneſs,
Will meet their full reward.

DUTCHESS.

                  Where is the friend
Who rung our diſmal knell?

DUKE.

                  Good, generous man!
Aſſur'd of death, yet careleſs of his life,
And anxious but for us, he is return'd,
To know what our brave leaders will determine——
Yet what can they determine but to die?
Our numbers poorly arm'd, undiſciplin'd,
May fight and fall with deſperate obſtinacy,
For valour can no more——But, oh Louiſa!
Friends, country, life itſelf, all loſt ſeem little;
One ſharp devouring grief conſumes the reſt,
And makes thee all its object.

DUTCHESS.

                  My dear huſband!
Theſe ſoft endearments, this exceſs of fondneſs,
Strike deeper to my ſoul, than all the pangs
The ſubtleſt vengeance cou'd contrive to wound me.
Oh fly me, hate me, call me murdereſs;
'Tis I have driven thee to this precipice,
I urge the ruffian hand of law to ſeize thee,
I drag thee to the block,——I lift the axe,
(Oh agony) Louiſa dooms thee dead!

DUKE.

DUKE.

—'Tis anguish infupportable to hear thee
Add felf-upbraidings to our mifery.
Thou my deftroyer! No my beft Louifa,
Thou art my guardian angel.——At this hour,
This dreadful hour, 'tis fafety to be near thee.
Thofe daftards who betray'd our brave defign,
That bafenefs which no caution cou'd prevent,
Nor wifdom cou'd forefee, 'twas that undid us.
I will not curfe them—Yet I fwear by honour,
Thus hunted to the utmoft verge of fate,
Without one ray of hope to cheer the danger,
I wou'd not barter this dire certainty,
For that ignoble life thofe bad men purchafe
By perfidy and vilenefs——

DUTCHESS.

Oh two fuch——
But indignation wants a tongue to name them.
How was their fury thunder'd on our fide!
Their youthful veins full of Patrician blood
Infulted by Velafquez—ftript by Spain
Of all the ancient honours of their houfe;
Sworn at the altar to affert this caufe
By holieft adjurations :—Yet thefe two
To turn apoftates—Can this fleeting breath,
This tranfitory, frail, uncertain being,
Be worth fo vaft a ranfom?

DUKE.

Yes, to cowards,
Such ever be the profelytes of Spain,——
Leave them to fcorn.——Fain wou'd I turn my thoughts
From this bad world——fhake off the clogs of earth,
And for that great tribunal, arm my foul,
Where Heaven, not Spain, muft judge me—but in vain ;
My foften'd mind ftill hangs on thofe bleft days,
Thofe years of fweet tranquility and peace,

When

When smiling morn but wak'd us to new joys,
And love at night shed blessings on our pillow.

DUTCHESS.

These hours are fled, and never can return.
'Tis Heaven's high will, and be that will obeyed.
The retrospect of past felicity
Plucks not the barbed arrow from the wound,
But makes it rankle deeper.—Come my Juan,
Here bid adieu to this infectious grief,
Let's knit our constancy to meet the trial;
Shall we be bold in words, mere moral talkers?
Declaim with pedant tongue in virtue's praise,
Yet find no comfort, no support within
From her bright energy?—It comes—it comes,
I feel my breast dilate—The phantom, death,
Shrinks at the radiant vision—bright ey'd hope
Bids us aspire, and points the shining throne.—
—Spain, I defy thee!

DUKE.

            O would she hew the elm,
And spare the tender vine—This stubborn trunk
Shou'd brave her fury.   Here is royal blood,
And blood long thirsted for.—They cannot dare,
Insatiate as they are, remorseless, savage,
With sacrilegious hands to violate
This beauteous sanctuary.—Let me not think.
Distraction—horror—Oh it splits my brain,
Rends every vital string, and tears my heart.
Mercy can grant no more—nor I petition,
Than to fall dead this instant and forget it.
I look towards Heaven in vain.—Gape wide, O earth,
And bury, bury deep this load of anguish.

DUTCHESS.

D U T C H E S S.

Be not fo loft.——Hear, Oh hear me Juan,
My lord, my life, my love.—— Wilt thou not fpeak ?
He heeds me not.——What fhall I fay to move him ?
For pity's fake look up.——Oh think Braganza,
Cou'd Spain behold thee thus—

D U K E.

Oh no, Louifa,
No eye fhall fee me melt.——I will be calm,
Still, filent, motionlefs.——Oh tough, tough heart,
Wou'd I could weep to eafe thee——

D U T C H E S S.

Here, weep here,
Pour the warm ftream into this faithful breaft,
Thy forrows here fhall find a kindred fource,
Which flows for every tear with drops of blood.
Now fummon all thy foul.——Behold, he comes
To thunder our irrevocable doom.

Enter R I B I R O.

R I B I R O

O for an angel's organ to proclaim
Such gratulations as no tongue can fpeak,
Nor mortal breaft conceive—joy, boundlefs joy.

D U K E.

Am I awake ?——Thou can'ft not mean to mock me.

R I B I R O.

I fhall go wild with tranfport.——On my knee
I beg you to forgive the cruel fhock
This tongue (Heaven knows with what fevere reluctance)
So lately gave to all your deareft hopes.

H   D U K E.

DUKE.

No, let me take that posture : for I swear,
Tho' yet I know not why, my lighten'd heart
Beats freer, and seems eas'd of half its burthen.
—Forgive my strong impatience—quickly tell me.

RIBIRO.

Still ignorant of our intended vengeance,
Velasquez is return'd.—Our gallant friends
Were wrong'd by rash suspicion.—

DUKE.

Heard I right?
Or is't illusion all? *(embracing him)* Thus let me thank thee.
Louisa then is safe —Fountain of mercy!
These late despairing arms again enfold her,
My Queen, my love, my wife!—

DUTCHESS.

Flow, flow my tears;
Take, bounteous lord of all, this melting tribute,
My heart can give no more for all thy goodness.

DUKE.

And now disclose this wonder.

RIBIRO.

Thus, my lord,
When at the appointed time, our two brave friends
Were hast'ning to Almada, near the square,
Velasquez and his followers cross'd their steps,
Their course seem'd towards the river;—struck with fear,
And ignorant what cause at that late hour
Cou'd draw him from the palace; straight they chang'd
Their first intent of joining our assembly,
And unobserv'd pursu'd the attending train.

I   Think

Think what thefe brave men fuffer'd when they faw
The tyrant climb his barge, and pufh from fhore.
Their fwords were half unfheath'd, both half refolv'd
To rufh at once, and pierce him to the heart.
—But prudence, or our fortune check'd their hands.

DUKE.

It had been certain ruin—but go on—

RIBIRO.

An inftant pafs'd in thought, they feiz'd a boat,
And following, anxious hung on all his motions :
Mendoza faw them thus—then hurrying back,
Fill'd us with confternation at the tidings.

DUTCHESS.

Nor was it ftrange—it wore a dreadful afpect ;
But fear interprets all things to its danger.

RIBIRO.

He crofs'd the river where Jago's fort
Commands the narrowing ftream. The governor
Attended at the gate, a while there pafs'd
In fhort but earneft converfe, they took leave,
With hafty ftrides Velafquez reimbark'd ;
The veffel, to the fhore fhe left, return'd,
And her proud mafter fought again the palace.

DUTCHESS.

Cou'd not our valiant friends difcover ought
That might reveal his purpofe ?

RIBIRO.

Madam—No.
To have enquir'd too near were dangerous
Befides, their hafte to reaffure our hopes
Prefs'd their return—But thus we may refolve :
He apprehends fome danger imminent.

He sees above his head the gathering cloud,
But knows not when 'twill burst in thunder on him.

D U K E.

Thanks, gentle friend——Alas, I tremble still ;
As just escap'd from shipwreck, I look round,
And tho' I tread on earth,——firm, solid earth
See with broad eye the threatning surge far off,
Scarce can I credit my conflicting sense
Or trust our preservation——

D U T C H E S S.

Thy glad tale
Has rais'd me from the gulph of black despair,
Even to the topmost pinnacle of joy.
Yes, we shall conquer — All these dangers past
Will serve but to enrich the future story.
Our children's children shall recount each fear,
And from the mingled texture of our lives,
Learn to revere that sacred Providence
That guides the strife of virtue.

D U K E.

O Louisa !
I thought I knew the extent of all my fondness,
That long acquaintance with thy wondrous virtue
Had given thee such dominion o'er my soul,
Time cou'd not add to my transcendent passion.
But when the danger came, it wak'd new fires,
Presented thee in softer loveliness,
And twin'd thee closer here.

R I B I R O.

My Lord, ere this
Our friends expect me.——

D U K E.

D U K E.

Let us fly to meet them.
I long to pour into their generous breasts
My cordial greeting.

D U T C H E S S.

Go my dearest Juan,
To them and all commend me; such rare zeal
Merits more recompence than our poor thanks
Can at the best requite. For souls like theirs
Ill brook the indignity of foul surmise;
And virtue wrong'd demands a double homage.

[Exit Dutchess.

D U K E.

If the good augury of my breast deceive not,
No more such terrors will appal our souls,
But guilt alone shall tremble——Come, Ribiro. [Exeunt.

SCENE changes to the Castle of A L M A D A.

ALMADA and several conspirators as before, with MELLO
and RODERIC.

A L M A D A.

Again our hopes revive——The unloaded stem
Shakes the wet tempest from its vigorous head,
And rears the swelling harvest to our sight.

M E N D O Z A.

After the chillings of this aguish fear,
Methinks I breathe more free——the vital stream
In sprightlier tides flows through its wonted course,
Warms my whole frame and doubly mans my heart.

A L M A D A.

A L M A D A.

And may the generous ardor spread to all——
Observe me friends,——our numbers must divide
Into four equal bands, all to attack
At the bell's signal the four palace gates.
So every passage barr'd, the foe in vain
May strive to unite and overwhelm our force.
Myself with the brave few, who have sworn to follow,
Will rush impetuous on the German guard,
Who at the northern entrance hold their station.
——The fort be Roderic and Mello's care,
With Ferdinand, Henriquez, and Antonio.
——Mendoza, Carlos, and their gallant troop
Must seize the regent Margaret, and secure
The counsellors of Spain as hostages
For the surrender of the citadel.

M E N D O Z A.

Letters to every province are dispers'd
Importing this great change, and all are ready
To shake to earth the intolerable yoke.
Nay distant India, in her sultry mines
Shall hear the chearful sound of liberty;
Again fair commerce welcom'd to our shore,
Shall loose her swelling canvas to the winds,
And golden Tagus heave once more to meet her.
But see the Duke.——

Enter DUKE.

A L M A D A.

Your unexpected presence,
Like a propitious omen cheers the night,
And gives a royal sanction to this meeting.

D U K E.

My wish surpass'd my speed——A call like this
Might imp the tardiness of feeble age.

The

The general perfeverance in our caufe
Tranfcends all gratitude——but thefe wrong'd virtues——
[*To Mello and Roderic.*

M E L L O.

Pray forbear;
The painful error brought its punifhment,
Ribiro bore our duties to your grace.

D U K E.

He did, and foon will join us——On our way
He left me with defign once more to view
The pofture of the guards,——for ftill we fear
Some dark impending mifchief from Velafquez.

A L M A D A.

Whatever fortune waits upon our fwords,
Your highnefs muft not fhare the common hazard ;
Left in the tumult fome inglorious chance
Deprive your country of its laft beft bulwark.

D U K E.

And fhou'd I merit to be call'd her bulwark,
Or rank with men like you.——cou'd I fubmit
To hear, and not partake the glorious danger ?

A L M A D A.

Pray be advis'd——in this I muft command.

D U K E-

Then be it fo——but yet fhou'd ought betide
To claim the interest of thy prince's arm,
I cannot wrong our friendfhip to fufpect
You will forbear my fummons to the field.

A L M A D A.

Truft your Almada——Lo ! the night wears faft ;
Nor are our fcatter'd numbers yet return'd.

D U K E.

DUKE.

Welcome Ribiro! What intelligence?

Enter R I B I R O.

R I B I R O.

The worst if we delay——Oh had your eyes
Beheld the sight that blasted mine.

DUKE.

What fight?

R I B I R O.

Lemos is seiz'd this moment——and Pizarro,
The ready tool of fell Velasquez' crimes,
Leads him to prison.

DUKE.

Soon we'll wrench the gates,
And from their gloomy caverns draw to light
All that remains of those unhappy men,
Whom unarraign'd unheard the tyrants nod
Consign'd to horrors nature shakes to think of.

A L M A D A.

His triumph will be short——The subtle fiend
May league with hell to thwart us——but in vain;
His fate or ours must quickly be decided.

R I B I R O.

Even now it seems his demon whispers him
His audit is at hand and scares his soul.
Anxious at this late hour, he walks his chamber,
Nor seeks the season's rest——and still more strange
The palace guards stretch'd by their glimmering fires,
Their arms cast by, lye wrapt in thoughtless sleep,

DUKE.

D U K E.

Anon we'll roufe them with fo loud a peal,
That death's dull ear fhall hear it.

A L M A D A.

Corea!
Soon as our work begins, your hardy tribes
Muft thro' the ftreets proclaim Don Juan King.
Prefs towards the palace; fhou'd our friends give ground,
Suftain their fainting ftrength.

C O R E A.

We will not fail.

A L M A D A.

The general fuffrage to thy fword, Ribiro,
Commits our mafter work; a deed fo envied
That ev'ry trenchant fteel of Portugal
(Did not thy gallant zeal demand it firft)
Would ftrike to fhare the glory.

R I B I R O.

(*Pointing to his fword.*) This fhall thank you,
And if it reek not with his hated blood
Exchange it for a diftaff.

A L M A D A.

Friends, I mean not
By gloomy prefage to allay your ardor.
We muft not look to fortune in this caufe:
But on ourfelves rely for fure fuccefs.
The leaft diforder in our bold approach,
The leaft repulfe may drive our engine back.
One brave man's rafhnefs, or one coward's fear,
Turns all our faireft hopes to fhame and ruin.

I

D U K E.

DUKE.

Now to our ftations——Yet ere we depart
This honeft pledge, the foldier's fhort embrace.
The fweet remembrance, if we fall for freedom,
Will more than foften half the pains of dying;
But if we meet, in ftronger clafps renew'd,
Will double all the joys of victory.

End of the Fourth A C T.

A C T

A C T   V.

S C E N E   I.

The Apartments of V E L A S Q U E Z *in the royal Palace.*

V E L A S Q U E'Z *alone.*

WHY am I haunted by these phantom fears?
It cannot be my fate. 'Tis nature's weakness:
The spirits rais'd too high, like billows puff'd
By sudden storms, lift up our little bark,
Then slipping from their burthen, sink as fast,
And leave it wreck'd and found'ring.

Enter P I Z A R R O.

V E L A S Q U E Z.

Have you, as I commanded, question'd Lemos?

P I Z A R R O.

Just now I left him.

V E L A S Q U E Z.

Has the slave confess'd?

P I Z A R R O.

With sullen calmness he defies your power,
Or answers but with scorn.

V E L A S Q U E Z.

We'll find the means
To make him speak more plainly, to bring down

I 2

Th.

This daring spirit—He is dangerous;
And under the fair mask of public virtue,
Combines with proud Almada and the rest
In dark confed'racy against my state.

P I Z A R R O.

He is, my Lord, the master-spring that moves
The factious populace.

V E L A S Q U E Z.

I know it well,
But I have ta'en such care as shall unhinge
Their ill-contriv'd designs.   Ere noon to-morrow,
Don Garcia, with the Spanish veterans
From Saint Jago's fortress, shall pour in
And bend these stubborn necks to due obedience.
How will their disappointed fury rave
To find their royal demagogue, Braganza,
The idol their vain worship rais'd so high,
Low levell'd with the earth.——I wonder much
Ramirez not returns——Night's latest watch
Will soon be told.

P I Z A R R O.

Perhaps he but delays
(For better welcome) to behold the effect
Of the dire venom, and to glad your ears
By telling how your enemy expir'd.

V E L A S Q U E Z.

It may be so, I cannot doubt the effect;
Poison administer'd will do its work,
And this most speedily; 'tis swift perdition.
Yet, tho' this hour cuts off my greatest foe,
If my firm soul were capable of fear,
I might distrust the promise of my fortunes.

PIZARRO.

Wherefore, my Lord?

VELASQUEZ.

I almoſt bluſh to tell it,
Tir'd with the travail of this anxious night,
I threw me on my couch, and try'd to reſt ;
I try'd in vain——my vexed lids ſcarce clos'd ;
Or when a momentary ſlumber ſeal'd them,
Strange viſions ſwam before their twilight ſenſe :
——But why retrace the hideous phantaſy ?
Yet ſtill it hovers round me, ſtill remains
A fearful reverence of the paſt illuſion.

PIZARRO.

Such reverence but degrades a noble mind,
And ſinks its vigour to an infant's weakneſs.
Beldams and prieſts infuſe theſe idle fears,
And turn the milk of nature to its bane. [*Noiſe at a diſtance.*

VELASQUEZ.

Heard you that noiſe? Didſt thou not mark, Pizarro?
The monk has kept his word—'Tis Juan's knell :
His followers who ſhouted him at noon,
Now wail his death.——My genius now has room ;
Their ſorrows are my triumph, and proclaim
Aſſur'd ſucceſs to my aſpiring ſoul.

PIZARRO.

Sure 'tis the din of claſhing arms——again——
It comes this way—

Enter OFFICER *with his ſword drawn,*

VELASQUEZ.

Ha ! bleeding—ſpeak
Know you the cauſe ?——Speak, inſtant, ſpeak—

OFFICER.

O F F I C E R.

Too well!
The raging multitude have forc'd their way;
Their cry is, Where's the tyrant?—Where's Velafquez?
Don Juan's at their head, and guides the ftorm.

V E L A S Q U E Z.

Juan alive! eternal filence feize thee!
Impoffible!

O F F I C E R.

Thefe eyes, my Lord, beheld him——
Saw his rais'd arm——

V E L A S Q U E Z.

Ha! am I then betray'd!
Perdition catch Ramirez——You, Pizarro,
Collect my fcatter'd train——I'll forth, and meet
The rebel's fword.

P I Z A R R O.

Be not fo rafh,
Nor venture fingly——   [Exit VELASQUEZ.

O F F I C E R.

He rufhes on his death.
Two of my foldiers are already flain,
Striving to bar the outward palace gates;
Where like a tide the frantic people prefs,
Bearing down all before them.

P I Z A R R O.

Hence, begone;
The uproar's louder——Wake the fleeping grooms——
Bid them bring arms——Alarm the magiftrates——
Send to the guard and draw them to the fquare.
[Exit OFFICER.

Re-enter

Re-enter VELASQUEZ.

VELASQUEZ.

Ruin'd! undone! all's loft——the ftreets are throng'd
With raging citizens——A furious band
Of armed Portugueze juft now are mounting,
Fate's bloody book is open'd ; and I read
My dreadful doom : yet I'll not tamely yield,
But grapple to the laft with deftiny.

PIZARRO.

All is not loft——perhaps fome means are left.

VELASQUEZ.

Juft at the gate I met the daftard monk
Struggling for entrance——fcarce his breath fuffic'd
To tell me that our purpofe had mifcarried,
And Juan lives——I ftabb'd him to the heart,
The beft reward for unperforming fear.

PIZARRO.

Think not of him——but fave yourfelf by flight.

VELASQUEZ.

Where can I fly ?——I am befet, devoted——
Our foes like famifh'd blood-hounds are abroad,
And have us in the wind.

PIZARRO.

            Refolve at once.——
The poftern's yet unforc'd, that way efcape,
Difguife yourfelf, and fly to Juan's palace.
'Tis but the terrace length——Implore his mercy ;
It is the foolifh weaknefs of his nature
To fpare where he may punifh.

VELASQUEZ.

VELASQUEZ.

                  Ak my life!
No, rather let me perish—Hold—his wife—
Perhaps alone, unguarded—If I fall,
I'll leave a scorpion in the traitor's breast,
Shall make him curse the hour he rous'd my fury.   [*Exit*

PIZARRO *alone.*

  Now let the tempest rise—Oh, fickle fortune!
This moment mounted to thy giddy top,
Now whirl'd to earth and groveling—Hark—they come.

RIBIRO *(entering with others.)*

  Search all the chambers—If the villain 'scape
Our work's but half accomplish'd—

PIZARRO.

                    Pass no farther.

RIBIRO.

This is the tyrant's bosom counsellor.
Where is thy master, Spaniard?

PIZARRO.

                Safe, I hope,
From lawless rage like thine, and still will live
To punish this outrageous violence.

RIBIRO.

  Insolent slave—And yet I like thy courage.
'Tis vain to strive, deliver up thy sword.
I will not force thee to betray thy master,
Perfidious as he is—Even in a foe
I can discern a virtue, and esteem it.
Gonsalez, guard him safe—the rest disperse,
And leave no place unsearch'd—He must be found:
But by your loves I charge you kill him not.
Rob not **my sword, but leave that stroke for me.**
                      [*Exeunt severally.*

SCENE *changes to the Duke of* B R A G A N Z A'S *Palace. Enter* DUTCHESS, *an Attendant following.*

D U T C H E S S.

No, Ines, no, I love my husband much,
But more his honour. Cou'd I press his stay
In tame inaction here to wait the event,
While almost in his sight, his crown and glory
Hung on the doubtful fate of others swords?
Wou'd he have heard me? No, I knew him better.
Soon as Almada's danger reach'd his ear,
Who twice repuls'd cou'd scarce renew the charge,
(Swift as a javelin cuts the whistling air)
He snatch'd his sword, and breaking from my arms,
Rush'd to the fight, and join'd the warring throng.

I N E S.

That favouring power which has so oft preserv'd,
Will not forsake him now.

D U T C H E S S.

O grant it Heaven!
Go, Ines, to the terrace, and observe
If any friend (for sure I may expect it)
Bring tidings from my husband.   [*Exit Ines.*
                              Would this arm,
This feeble arm had strength to second him!
The conflict here is worse.——My restless heart,
Swell'd with eventful expectation, throbs
And feels its bounds too narrow.——Fear on fear,
Like light reflected from the dancing wave,
Visits all places, but can rest in none.
The distant shouts, that break the morning sky,
Lift up a while my mounting thoughts to Heaven,
Then sinking, leave them to fall down as low,
In boding apprehension.——Welcome, welcome?
                    K   *Enter*

Enter MENDOZA.

What of my lord?

MENDOZA.

He bad me fly to greet you;
Himself a while detain'd to stop the rage
Of cruelty and carnage.

DUTCHESS.

He returns
Unhurt, victorious to these happy arms?

MENDOZA.

All, all your fondest wish cou'd form he brings,
Crown, conquest, all.—Oppression is no more,
Pierc'd by a thousand wounds the giant dies,
While free-born men with fearless gaze walk round,
And view the monster's bulk.

DUTCHESS.

I wou'd know more.—
Was it a dear bought triumph? Must we mourn
The fall of many friends?

MENDOZA.

Scarce one of note
But lives to share our joy.—The regent seiz'd,
Gave orders for the citadel's surrender,
To save the threaten'd lives of the whole council,
Whom sleeping we secur'd.—Poorly content
To obey her mandate, though he knew it forc'd,
The dastard governor resign'd his charge,
And struck the Austrian banner.—Such the power
Of Juan's royal name, and conquering arm.
The rest himself will tell.—I must return.—

Abroad

Abroad the wild commotion rages ftill ;
The King may want my fervice—Angels guard you.

[*Exit Mendoza.*

D U T C H E S S.

O fly, begone, lofe not a thought on me.
Now to thy reft, my foul, thy pray'rs are heard.
From this white hour the bright revolving fun
With kinder beams fhall view this fmiling land ;
A grateful people, by my Juan's arm,
Refcued from fhameful bonds, fhall blefs his name,
And own him their preferver. *(Enter Ines.)* From my lord ?

I N E S.

Madam, not yet——A ftranger at the gate,
Difguis'd, and almoft breathlefs with his fears,
With earneft importunity entreats
He may have leave to caft him at your feet.
His accents mov'd me much ; he feems afflicted.

D U T C H E S S.

Some wretch efcap'd from the purfuer's rage,
And flies for fhelter here.—Yes, let him come.   [*Exit Ines.*

D U T C H E S S *alone.*

Wou'd I cou'd fave them all—my woman's foul,
Forc'd from her place in this tumultuous fcene,
But ill fupports the affum'd feverity,
And finds her native feat in foft compaffion.

Enter V E L A S Q U E Z, *difguifd.*

Whoe'er thou art, be fafe.—The greedy fword
Will have enough of death, and well may fpare
One fugitive, who fhuns its cruel edge
To wait the ftroke of nature.—Truft thy fafety.—
Why do thy doubtful eyes fo oft look round ?
Here are no enemies.—My word is pafs'd

~~i~~   Inviolable

Inviolable as recorded oaths.———
——Methinks I have seen that face.——Say, art thou not——

V E L A S Q U E Z.

The man you most shou'd fear, most hate.

D U T C H E S S.

Velasquez!

V E L A S Q U E Z.

Yes, that devoted wretch, the lost Velasquez;
From the high top of proud prosperity,
Sunk to this ignominy.

D U T C H E S S.

Presumptuous man!
If mercy cou'd know bounds, thy monstrous crimes
Almost exceed them.——Speak then, what cou'd urge thee
To seek the shelter of this hostile roof,
And trust a virtue to thy soul a stranger?

V E L A S Q U E Z.

Fate left no second choice.——Close at my heels
Revenge and death insatiably pursu'd;
Fear lent me speed, and this way wing'd my flight.
Why flash those eyes with anger?——Royal lady!
Fortune has stripp'd me of the power to injure;
A stingless serpent, a poor fang-drawn lion,
Fitter for scorn than terror.——

D U T C H E S S.

Thou art fallen!
Yet let me not insult thy alter'd state,
By pity or upbraiding.——If thy life
Be worth the acceptance——take it——and hereafter
Wash out the foulness of thy former deeds
By penitence and better purposes. [*shouts without.*]

The

These joyful sounds proclaim my Juan near
(*To Velasquez*)—Retire a while till I prepare my lord
To shield thee from the angry nobles rage.
All were combin'd to take thy forfeit life.——

DUKE *without.*

Throw wide the palace gates—Let all have entrance.

DUTCHESS.

His well-known voice—'Tis he, 'tis he himself!

DUKE *without.*

Where is my Queen?

DUTCHESS.

       Quick let me fly to meet him,
Fly to my hero's breast.——
     [*Velasquez seizes her and draws a dagger.*

VELASQUEZ.

      Hold, madam, hold,
Thus I arrest your transports.

DUTCHESS.

     Barbarian! monster!

DUKE *entering.*

What sounds are these? Horror! Inhuman slave?
Turn thy fell pogniard here

VELASQUEZ.

      Approach not, stir not.
Or by the blackest furies hell e'er loos'd,
This dagger drinks her blood.

               DUKE

DUKE.

        See, I obey,
I breathe not, stir not, I am rooted here.
Here will I grow for ages.

DUTCHESS.

        Oh my Juan!

DUKE.

O horrible! Does Juan live for this?
Curs'd be the fatal fire that led my steps
To follow false ambition, while I left
To lurking robbers an unguarded prize;
This gem more worth than crowns or worlds can ransom

VELASQUEZ.

Take back a name more foul, thou dark usurper
Was it for this, thy unsuspecting prince
With lavish bounty, to thy faithless hand
Trusted his royal functions? Thus to arm
'Gainst his own breast, thy black ingratitude.

DUKE.

Must I endure it?

DUTCHESS.

        Out! false hypocrite!
Thy tyrants snares were found, his flimsy nets
To catch that precious life long since unravel'd,
Thy conscious cheek avows it.

VELASQUEZ.

        Be it so. —

DUTCHESS.

Coward! Perfidious coward! Is it thus,
Thus you require——

                VELAS-

V E L A S Q U E Z.

Thy foolish pity——thus——
Hear me thou rebel——Is this woman dear?

D U K E.

O heavens!

V E L A S Q U E Z.

Thy ftraining eyes, thy agonizing heart,
Thy life's inglorious dotage all proclaim it.

D U T C H E S S.

Peace, devil, peace, nor wound his generous foul
By taunts that fiends might bluth at.

D U K E.

Speak thy purpofe.

V E L A S Q U E Z.

Then briefly thus — call off thy traiterous guards,
——The fruits of thy foul treafon, every poft,
Seiz'd by the midnight plots, thy rebel arms
Reftore again to Spain——Back to the palace
Give me fave conduct——To thy oaths I truft not;
It muft be done this inftant——leave my power
To intercede with Spain for thy full pardon,
And grace to all, whom thy ill-ftarr'd ambition
Led to this bafe revolt——Elfe, by my rage!
The boiling rage that works my foul to frenzy,
Thou fhalt behold this beauteous bofom gor'd,
All over gafh'd and mangled

D U T C H E S S.

Strike this inftant!

D U K E.

Hold, ruffian, hold!

DUCHESS.

DUTCHESS.

Give me a thousand deaths;
Here let me fall a glorious sacrifice,
Rather than buy my life by such dishonour.
(*To the Duke*) If thy fond love accept these shameful terms,
That moment is my last—these hands shall end me.
(*To Velasquez*) Blood thirsty tyger, glut thy fury here.

VELASQUEZ.

Her courage blasts my purpose (*aside*) dost thou brave me

DUTCHESS.

Defy thee—yes—feel, do I shrink or tremble?
Serene undaunted will I meet the blow;
But ev'ry drop that stains thy reeking hands,
In thy last pangs shall cry for vengeance on thee.
Furies shall seize thee, shake their scorpion whips,
And in thy deafen'd ears still hollow, murder.

VELASQUEZ.

No more—Resolve—(*To the Duke.*)—Not Heaven itself
can save her.
Ha! darkness cover me! he still alive!
Fate thou hast caught me—Every hope is lost.

(*Enter Ramirez wounded, Almada, Ribiro, Mendoza and others following—The Duke and Dutchess run to each others arms—Velasquez is seized.*)

DUKE.

I have thee once again, my heart's best treasure,
Sav'd from the vulture's talons—O dire fiend!

VELAS-

VELASQUEZ.

Unhand me—No—though earth and hell confpire.

DUTCHESS.

Blafphemer, down! and own a power above thee!

RIBIRO.

Secure this monfter—Read this paper, madam.
Returning from the charge we found that wretch
Stretch'd in our way and welt'ring in his blood;
Earneft he beg'd we fhou'd commit to note
Thefe few fhort words, and bear them to the Duke.
That done, he dragg'd his bleeding body on,
And came to die before him.

DUKE.

       Oh, Ramirez!
Ev'n in this day of joy my heart runs o'er
With forrow for thy fate—What cruel hand?

RAMIREZ.

—A villain's hand, yet Heaven directed it.
I have not ftrength to publifh all my fhame,
That roll contains it—This wide gaping wound,
My deep remorfe, may expiate my crime;
But, Oh! that tempter—

DUKE.

      Ha! he faints, fupport him.
Thy crime, what crime?

RAMIREZ.

      Thy happier ftar prevail'd,
Elfe, hadft thou died even by the pious act
That feals our peace above.

DUKE.

      Merciful powers!
    L   RAMIREZ.

R A M I R E Z.

Yet ere I fink, fpeak comfort to my foul,
And blefs me with forgivenefs.

D U K E.

Take it freely.

R A M I R E Z.

Enongh, I die contented.   [*He is led off*

D U T C H E S S.

O my Juan,
Perufe that tale and wonder——Impious wretch,
Well might my heart ftand ftill——my blood run cold,
And ftruggling nature murmur ftrong reluctance
Againft my foolifh pity——While I meant
To ftep between thee and the brandifh'd bolt,
To refcue from the ftroke of righteous juftice
The foul fuborner of my hufband's murder.

V E L A S Q U E Z.

Curfe on the coward's fears prevented it!
Wither thefe finews that relax'd their hold,
And left thy feeble wing to foar above me.

D U K E.

Hence with that villa... drag him from my fight.——
Till aweful juftice doom his forfeit life,
Let heavieft chains fecure him——Hence, begone.

V E L A S Q U E Z.

Yes, in your gloomieft dungeons plunge me down.
Welcome congenial darknefs——Horrors hail!
No more thefe loathing eyes fhall view that fun,
Whofe iikfome beams light up thy pageant triumph.
                    [*He is led off by Ribiro and others.*

D U K E.

Thou ever prefent, all protecting power!
Thro' what dark clouds of thick involving danger
Thy watchful providence has led my fteps?
The imagin'd woes that funk me in defpair,
Thou mad'ft the wond'rous inftruments to fave me.

D U T C H E S S.

I feel, I own the high fupremacy—
Yet have I much to afk—Thy victory—

D U K E.

For that our thanks to this brave man are due.
He chofe the poft of danger, and expos'd
His dauntlefs breaft againft the ftubborn force
Of fteady northern courage.

A L M A D A.

     Twice was I down,
And twice my prince's valour refcued me.

D U K E.

For ever hallow'd be the well pois'd blade
That fav'd that reverend head.

D U T C H E S S.

Fortune was kind, Almada, to commit
Your fafety to the arm you taught to conquer.

A L M A D A.

Henceforth I more fhall prize that trifle life,
Since now I owe it to my fovereign's valour.

Enter R I B I R O.

R I B I R O.

Vengeance thy debt is paid—The tyrant's dead.

         DUKE.

DUKE.

Say'st thou? Velasquez!

RIBIRO.

                         Aye, what was Velasquez
Dispers'd and mangled by the people's rage,
In bloody fragments stains a thousand hands;
Like ravenous wolves by eager famine pinch'd,
With worrying fangs they dragg'd him from my grasp,
And in my sight tore out his reeking entrails.

DUKE.

His blood be on his head, and may his end,
Provok'd by crimes beyond the reach of pardon,
Strike terror to the souls of impious men,
Who own no God, but from his pow'r to punish.

THE END.